MATH 24/7

SHOPPING MATH

HELEN THOMPSON

Mason Crest

Mason Crest
450 Parkway Drive, Suite D
Broomall, PA 19008
www.masoncrest.com

Printed in the United States of America.

First printing
9 8 7 6 5 4 3 2 1

Series ISBN: 978-1-4222-2901-9
ISBN: 978-1-4222-2908-8
ebook ISBN: 978-1-4222-8919-8

The Library of Congress has cataloged the
        hardcopy format(s) as follows:

        Library of Congress Cataloging-in-Publication Data

Thompson, Helen, 1957-
 Shopping math / Helen Thompson.
    pages cm. – (Math 24/7)
 Audience: 10.
 Audience: Grade 4 to 6.
 Includes index.
    ISBN 978-1-4222-2908-8 (hardcover) – ISBN 978-1-4222-2901-9 (series) – ISBN 978-1-4222-8919-8 (ebook)
 1. Shopping–Mathematics–Juvenile literature. I. Title.
 TX335.5.T46 2014
 381.001'51–dc23
                    2013015667

Produced by Vestal Creative Services.
www.vestalcreative.com

Contents

INTRODUCTION

How would you define math? It's not as easy as you might think. We know math has to do with numbers. We often think of it as a part, if not the basis, for the sciences, especially natural science, engineering, and medicine. When we think of math, most of us imagine equations and blackboards, formulas and textbooks.

But math is actually far bigger than that. Think about examples like Polykleitos, the fifth-century Greek sculptor, who used math to sculpt the "perfect" male nude. Or remember Leonardo da Vinci? He used geometry—what he called "golden rectangles," rectangles whose dimensions were visually pleasing—to create his famous *Mona Lisa*.

Math and art? Yes, exactly! Mathematics is essential to disciplines as diverse as medicine and the fine arts. Counting, calculation, measurement, and the study of shapes and the motions of physical objects: all these are woven into music and games, science and architecture. In fact, math developed out of everyday necessity, as a way to talk about the world around us. Math gives us a way to perceive the real world—and then allows us to manipulate the world in practical ways.

For example, as soon as two people come together to build something, they need a language to talk about the materials they'll be working with and the object that they would like to build. Imagine trying to build something—anything—without a ruler, without any way of telling someone else a measurement, or even without being able to communicate what the thing will look like when it's done!

The truth is: We use math every day, even when we don't realize that we are. We use it when we go shopping, when we play sports, when we look at the clock, when we travel, when we run a business, and even when we cook. Whether we realize it or not, we use it in countless other ordinary activities as well. Math is pretty much a 24/7 activity!

And yet lots of us think we hate math. We imagine math as the practice of dusty, old college professors writing out calculations endlessly. We have this idea in our heads that math has nothing to do with real life, and we tell ourselves that it's something we don't need to worry about outside of math class, out there in the real world.

But here's the reality: Math helps us do better in many areas of life. Adults who don't understand basic math applications run into lots of problems. The Federal Reserve, for example, found that people who went bankrupt had an average of one and a half times more debt than their income—in other words, if they were making $24,000 per year, they had an average debt of $36,000. There's a basic subtraction problem there that should have told them they were in trouble long before they had to file for bankruptcy!

As an adult, your career—whatever it is—will depend in part on your ability to calculate mathematically. Without math skills, you won't be able to become a scientist or a nurse, an engineer or a computer specialist. You won't be able to get a business degree—or work as a waitress, a construction worker, or at a checkout counter.

Every kind of sport requires math too. From scoring to strategy, you need to understand math—so whether you want to watch a football game on television or become a first-class athlete yourself, math skills will improve your experience.

And then there's the world of computers. All businesses today—from farmers to factories, from restaurants to hair salons—have at least one computer. Gigabytes, data, spreadsheets, and programming all require math comprehension. Sure, there are a lot of automated math functions you can use on your computer, but you need to be able to understand how to use them, and you need to be able to understand the results.

This kind of math is a skill we realize we need only when we are in a situation where we are required to do a quick calculation. Then we sometimes end up scratching our heads, not quite sure how to apply the math we learned in school to the real-life scenario. The books in this series will give you practice applying math to real-life situations, so that you can be ahead of the game. They'll get you started—but to learn more, you'll have to pay attention in math class and do your homework. There's no way around that.

But for the rest of your life—pretty much 24/7—you'll be glad you did!

1
USING A
SHOPPING LIST

One of Mikayla's favorite things to do is to go shopping. It doesn't even matter what she's buying—clothes, groceries, books. Mikayla likes buying new stuff when she can, and she really likes picking out and buying presents for her family and friends.

Sometimes she can end up going overboard, though, and buying too much during a shopping trip. One of the things Mikayla does to help her not do that is make a shopping list. Making a shopping list helps keep her focused on getting what she needs, and not spending too much money. On her list, she **estimates** how much each item will cost, and then finds the total at the bottom. Then she knows how much she expects to spend. The next page shows an example of a shopping list Mikayla made before going to a department store.

Mikayla's shopping list:

Sunglasses, $15
Jeans, $20
Notebook, $3
Laundry detergent for Dad, $4.50
Present for Jon: Movie, $20
Birthday card for Jon, $2.50

All of Mikayla's estimates are either whole dollars, or dollars with 50 cents added on. That makes it easy to add up the estimates to get a good idea of how much she will spend on her shopping trip.

1. What is the total she estimates she will spend?

Then her dad reminds her to buy him some new headphones. She accidentally broke his, and promised to buy him some new ones. The headphones will cost $25.

2. Now how much does Mikayla estimate she will spend?

When Mikayla goes to the store, she finds that not all her estimates were exactly right.

This is what each of the items actually costs:

Sunglasses, $16.53
Jeans, $20.30
Notebook, $2.57
Laundry detergent, $4.10
Movie, $16.75
Birthday card, $2.16
Headphones, $24.86

3. How much will she end up paying?

4. Which of her estimates was closest? Which was farthest off?

9

2
BUDGETING

Before Mikayla checks out, she has to see if she can afford to buy everything. She is on a budget, because she doesn't have unlimited supplies of money! A budget is a plan of how to spend money. It includes how much money you have, what you need to buy, and what you want to buy.

Mikayla has a part-time job and makes a little money each week. She puts a lot of it in her **savings account**, though, so she doesn't spend it all. The rest she uses to first buy what she needs, and then what she wants.

Mikayla suspects she can't afford to buy everything in her basket. Look at the next page to decide what she can keep and what she has to put back.

Mikayla makes a list in her head that looks like this:

Needs (Have to buy)
Notebook, $2.57
Laundry detergent, $4.10
Movie (present), $16.75
Birthday card, $2.16
Headphones, $24.86

Wants (Don't have to buy)
Sunglasses, $16.53
Jeans, $20.30

1. If she only buys what she needs, how much would she spend?

Mikayla makes $40 babysitting for a neighbor every week, plus $6 an hour for walking another neighbor's dog, which she usually does for 4 hours a week.

2. How much does she make every week?

She sets aside 40% of her money to spend and puts the rest in her savings account for later.

Percents are parts out of 100. 40% is like saying 40 parts out of 100. To figure out how much 40% of her weekly income is, first move the decimal point in 40 over to the left two places to change it into a decimal number. Then multiply how much Mikayla makes a week by the decimal:

40% = .40
.40 x weekly income = spending money

3. How much does she have to spend every week?

Right now, Mikayla has two weeks' worth of money to spend.

4. How much does she have? Does she have enough to buy what she needs on her shopping list?

5. Does she have enough to also buy one of the items she wants? Could she buy both of them?

3
PARKING

On another shopping trip, Mikayla and her friends go to the mall. One of her friends, Janine, has a car and drives them all to the mall. They circle around the parking lot for a while, looking for a space. They finally find one and pull in. But when Mikayla goes to open the passenger side door, she can't get out! The space is too narrow.

Even before they step foot into the mall, math is involved in their shopping trip. The parking lot is a great place to explore geometry, the math of size and space. The next pages will give you a better understanding of parking-lot geometry.

When Janine pulled into the parking space, she didn't realize there wasn't quite enough room for everyone to get out easily.

Find the area of the space Janine needed to park in so that there was enough room for both the car and the passengers getting out.

The equation for the area of a rectangle is:

$$A = \text{length} \times \text{width}.$$

Janine's car is **approximately** 14 feet and 9 inches long and 6 feet and 2 inches wide. To find the area, you'll need to remember there are 12 inches in 1 foot.

1. First, convert the length and width to inches:

2. Next, plug those numbers into the area formula. What is the area of the car in square inches?

But that isn't all the room they need. They also need 1 foot of space on either side of the car to be able to open the doors and get out. This extra space has to be added to the width of the car. The length will stay the same.

3. How much extra space in inches do they need?

4. What is the total width they now need for the parking space?

You can find the new, bigger area they will need for the parking space using the same area equation.

5. What is the new area they need? How much bigger is it than the area the car takes up?

4
SALES TAX

At the first store Mikayla and her friends go into, Mikayla finds the perfect dress. It's pretty expensive, though. The tag says it is $60. Mikayla isn't sure she has enough money, but she really loves the dress. She is willing to spend all the money she brought on it, even though it would mean she couldn't buy anything else.

Then Janine reminds her that she has to add in sales tax to the price on the tag. Sales tax is the money the government collects on purchases. The government uses the sales tax money—and the other taxes it collects—to provide protection and services to people, like police, parks, and schools. The sales tax **rate** in Mikayla's state and county is 7.3%.

Now Mikayla really isn't sure if she can buy the dress. Should Mikayla buy the dress? Does she have enough money? You can figure it out with percents on the next page.

Mikayla has to count all the money she brought with her to know if buying the dress is even an option. She takes out her cash and counts:

One $20 bill
Two $10 bill
Three $5 bills
Eight $1 bills
3 quarters
2 dimes

1. How much does he have in total? Does she have enough to buy the dress without the sales tax?

Now figure out how much the dress would be with the sales tax added on. You know the tax is 7.3%. You can use several ways to calculate the price.

First, you can move the decimal point and multiply like you did in Chapter 2. Right now, you are just finding the amount of sales tax, not the total price of the dress.

2. What is 7.3% in decimal form?

3. What is the sales tax?

Another way to use percents is to cross multiply. A percent is a part out of 100, which you can compare to the relationship between the numbers you are using.

4.
$$\frac{7.3}{100} = \frac{X}{60}$$

100 x X = 7.3 x 60

X = (7.3 x 60) ÷ 100

Hopefully, you got the same answer using both methods! Now you can add the sales tax to the price tag and see what the total price for the dress is.

5. What is the total price? Can Mikayla afford it?

5

SPENDING CASH

Mikayla only uses cash to buy things when she goes shopping. She doesn't have any bank cards. Because her only money is the cash she has with her, she decides not to buy the dress. She can't afford it, and she doesn't really want to borrow money from her friends.

That means she still has $60 to spend if she wants. She still wants to buy jeans and sunglasses, which are the items she couldn't afford to buy on her shopping list when she went to the department store earlier. What can she buy? How should she divide up her money? Help her figure it out on the next page.

Mikayla finds a pair of jeans that have a tag saying $31.50.

1. How much are the jeans, including sales tax?

She buys the jeans and gives the cashier a $20 bill, two $10 bills, 3 quarters, and a dime.

2. How much change should she get?

Now she just wants to find sunglasses. However, she also wants to save a little bit to buy something in the food court with her friends. She estimates she will need $7 left over.

3. How much money does she have left to buy the sunglasses?

She shops around at a few more stores and finds some sunglasses for $12.99, not including tax.

4. How much will the sales tax be? Does she have enough money to buy the sunglasses?

Mikayla gives the cashier two $10 bills. The cashier hands back a $5 bill, three quarters, and a nickel.

5. Did she give back enough change? If not, how much more does she need to give Mikayla?

After her purchases, Mikayla reaches into her pocket and takes out all the money she has left. She has:

one $5 bill
three $1 bills
four quarters
two dimes
a penny

6. How much does she have left? Is it enough to buy something at the food court?

6

USING A
DEBIT CARD

Mikayla's friend Janine doesn't bring cash to the mall. Instead, she has a debit card. She set up a checking account with the bank, where she keeps all her spending money. Every time she **deposits** money in her checking account, she can use her debit card to make purchases.

She can also use her debit card with an ATM (Automated Teller Machine). She can **withdraw** cash from her account if she ends up needing it, or she can check how much money she has left in her account.

It's often harder to tell how much money you have left to spend in a checking account. You can't just look in your wallet like you can with cash. If you spend too much money, the bank will charge you a **fee**, and then you'll have to pay the bank. Having a debit card and checking account can make shopping easier, but they also come with some responsibilities!

Janine, like Mikayla, is also on a budget. She thinks she has $45 left in her checking account. If she spends more than that, the bank will charge her $30 for using more money than is in her account.

The first thing Janine buys is a pair of earrings for $5.67, with tax. She's pretty sure she has enough money for them in her account.

The next store she goes into takes cash only, and she wants to buy a scarf for $11.99. Janine only has her card, but she goes to an ATM for some cash. While she's there, she checks her balance, to see how much money she really has left. The ATM says she has $23.12 in her account, which is less than she thought she had.

1. What was her balance before she bought the earrings?

She wants to take out at least $11.99. The ATM only gives out money in **multiples** of $20.

2. What is the least amount of money Janine can take out of the ATM?

The ATM is also run by Bank A, but Janine has an account at Bank B. The ATM charges anyone not from Bank A $3.50 for using it.

3. How much money will she be taking from her checking account, including the ATM fee? Does she have enough money in her account?

In the end, she doesn't take out any money. But in the next store, which does take debit cards, she sees these things she wants (including sales tax):

Board game, $12.45
Shirt, $25.98
Wallet, $10.20
Computer case, $31.10

4. Which of these things can she afford, and which can she not afford?

7
USING A CREDIT CARD

Mikayla's friend Yi, who is also shopping with them, has a credit card. He has a part-time job, and likes to read about **finances**. He likes having a credit card, because it helps him understand money and shopping a little better.

Using a credit card is like borrowing money. You can make a purchase today and not have to use your own money to make your purchase. However, credit cards are not free money. You will have to pay the bank back in a few weeks. Credit cards are useful when you don't have enough money to buy something you really need right now, but you know you will have money for it a little later on. If you can't pay for your purchase later, though, you will go into debt. Find out how credit cards really work, and how Yi uses his, on the next page.

Yi needs to buy a new suit for a school dance. Suits are pretty expensive, but he likes to pay for things himself because he has a part-time job, and he likes to **manage** his money.

The trouble is, he doesn't have enough money right now. He only has $15 in his checking account.

The good news is that he is getting a paycheck next week for $80, and one the week after for $95. He likes to save $25 from each paycheck for the future.

Here are the suits Yi finds, and their price tags:

Suit 1: $99.99
Suit 2: $220.00
Suit 3: $115.30
Suit 4: $170.00
Suit 5: $105.60
Suit 6: $199.99

1. Can Yi pay for any of the suits with the money he has right now? Will he need to use his credit card?

2. Which of the suits could Yi pay off if he used all the money from both his paychecks and didn't save any money?

3. Which of the suits could Yi pay off if he used only the money from his paycheck next week?

4. Which of the suits could Yi pay off if he used only the money that was left from both paychecks after he put some aside for savings?

5. How much money would Yi have left from his paychecks if he put some aside for savings and also bought Suit 5? Don't forget to add on sales tax.

8
CLOTHES SIZING

Mikayla hasn't gone shopping in a few weeks. She has been saving up her money to buy some new jeans. She isn't quite sure what she wants yet, but her old jeans are wearing thin in the knees. It's time to buy some new ones.

When she gets to the store, she starts looking through the racks. She finds a couple styles she really likes and looks at the size tag. They have sizes on them she doesn't recognize! She isn't sure which ones she should take to the dressing room, so she goes and finds a store employee.

Sometimes when you are shopping for clothes, you will need to **convert** from one size system to another. In the United States, people may wear girls' sizes, boys' sizes, juniors' sizes, men's sizes, women's sizes, and more! Some clothes come in European sizes too, which are based on measurements. For jeans, European sizes are based on how big around your waist is in centimeters, which is the circumference of (distance around) your waist.

Mikayla usually wears juniors' sizes, but she has stumbled on jeans with women's and European sizes. Help her figure out what size she should try on.

Mikayla usually wears a size 9 in juniors' sizing, sometimes an 11. She can't find any juniors' sizes in this store, though, only women's and European sizes.

The store employee tells Mikayla she can convert from juniors' sizes to women's sizes in her head. Juniors' sizes come in odd numbers, and women's sizes come in even numbers. She just needs to subtract 3 from the juniors' size she normally wears.

1. Which women's sizes should Mikayla try on?

Then the store employee shows Mikayla the following sizing cart, to explain how European sizing works:

U.S. Juniors' size	European size
1	28
3	30
5	32
7	34
9	36
11	38
13	40
15	42

She explains that there are also odd numbers in between the even European sizes. So, a size 33 jean would **correspond** to a size 5½ in juniors' sizes.

The store employee takes out a tape measure and measures Mikayla's waist, which is 37.25 inches around.

Because Mikayla's waist isn't a whole number, she should round up and down to the nearest whole numbers to find out which sizes she should try on.

2. According to the chart, and your own math, which two European sizes should she try on?

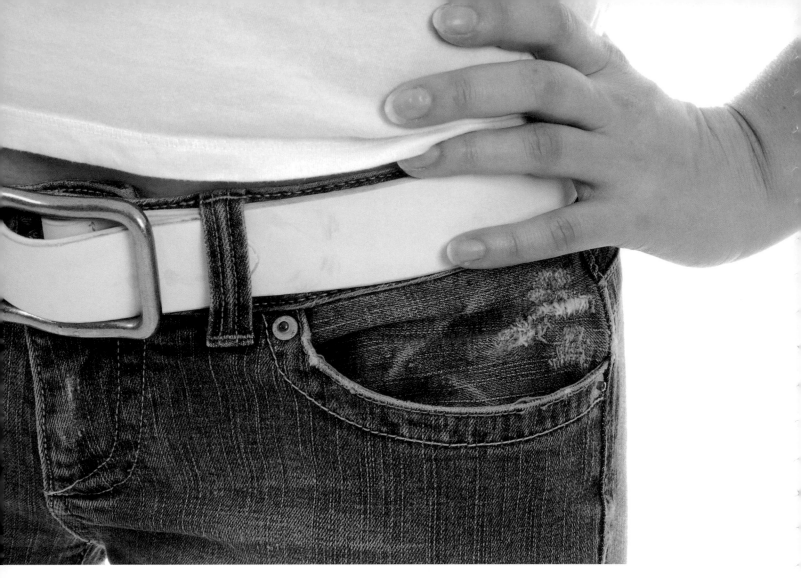

9
COST-PER-WEAR

Now that Mikayla has found the right jean size, she's ready to try on some and buy a pair. One way Mikayla can pick a pair of jeans is to think about the cost-per-wear. Mikayla will have to pay however much the jeans cost right at the store. Every time she wears them after that, she is getting some **value** out of them. If the jeans fit and she really likes them, she will wear them a lot. She might have paid a lot of money, but it was worth it because she wears them a lot. If the jeans don't fit and she doesn't like them, she will wear them only a couple times. She just paid a lot of money for something she doesn't wear.

Cost-per-wear is a way of thinking about buying clothes. You could also think of other items in terms of cost-per-use. How many times do you use a blanket? Or a video game? The more you use them, the more value you're getting out of them. Knowing how to calculate cost-per-wear can help you save lots of money over time.

The equation for cost-per-wear is:

price of the clothing ÷ how many times you wear the clothing

The units of cost-per-wear are dollars per wear. It's really very simple.

1. What would the cost-per-wear be if you paid $50 for a shirt, and you wore it 25 times?

Mikayla shops around for some jeans and finds 3 pairs she likes. Here are their prices, including sales tax:

Pair 1: $25
Pair 2: $14.50
Pair 3: $65

2. What is the order of these jeans from cheapest to most expensive?

Mikayla tries on Pair 1. They fit really well, and are the right length and style. She asks her friend Luisa's opinion, and she thinks they fit well too. Mikayla thinks she would wear them once a week for two years before they wore out.

Now figure out the cost-per-wear for Pair 1. First, figure out how many times she would wear them before they wore out. There are 52 weeks in a year, which will help you figure it out.

1 time a week x 52 weeks x 2 years = 104 times

Now plug the numbers into the cost-per-wear equation.

3. $25 ÷ 104 times =

Mikayla tries on the other two pairs. Pair 2 is cheap, but uncomfortable and doesn't quite fit right. If she bought them, she might only wear them once a month for a year. Pair 3 is really expensive and a designer brand, and fits about as well as Pair 1. She thinks she would wear them about the same amount.

4. What are the cost-per-wear numbers for the other two pairs?

Mikayla should buy the jeans with the best cost-per-wear value. That means the jeans that cost the least whenever she wears them—the lowest cost-per-wear number.

5. Which pair of jeans should Mikayla buy based on cost-per-wear? Why?

10
SALES
AND DISCOUNTS

Mikayla still has time to shop before she has to go home, so she heads over to the bookstore. She likes to read, but hasn't bought any new books in a while. The bookstore is having a big sale. Almost everything is discounted! Mikayla decides she has enough money to buy a few books.

Sales have a lot to do with percents and fractions. Once you figure out percents and fractions, you'll be able to find the best sales. Check out the next page to practice with sales and discounts.

The books on sale have colored labels on them that identify how much they're discounted. Here's the system:

Red: 5% off
Orange: 10% off
Yellow: 25% off
Green: 50% off
Blue: 75% off
Purple: 90% off

Mikayla doesn't necessarily want to wait till she gets to the cash register to find out how much the books cost. She can calculate their prices if she can change the percents into fractions.

Some common percents and their fraction **equivalents** are:

¼ = one-fourth = 25%
⅓ = one-third = 33%
½ = one-half = 50%
¾ = three-quarters = 75%

Sometimes it's easier to understand that 50%, for example, is just half of the price.

1. Can you figure out how much a book with a green tag that is $12 would cost after the discount?

2. How about a book with a yellow tag that costs $20?

Some of the percents are a little harder to calculate off the top of your head, like 90%. But if you ask yourself good questions, you can arrive at an approximate sales price. For example:

3. If book is $16 and 90% off, will it be more likely to cost $3 or $15? Why?

4. What will a $16 book that is 90% off really cost after the discount? Use any math you want to calculate the answer.

11

BUY-ONE-GET-ONE SALES

Mikayla finds a section of the bookstore that is selling books using a buy-one-get-one sale. On one shelf, if she buys one book, she gets another one on the same shelf free. On another shelf, if she buys one book, she gets another half off.

Buy-one-get-one sales can be good deals, but they can also make you waste your money. If you really only want to buy one thing, you might get tricked into buying another if you know you can buy it on sale.

Understanding buy-one-get-one sales can help you save money and get things you really need and want on sale. Turn to the next page to figure out how they work.

On the buy-one-get-one shelf, Mikayla finds a novel she really wants. It costs $23, but it has a blue sticker on it, so it's also on sale. She also finds a history book she wants to read, and it costs $14 with an orange sticker. (Turn back to page X to see what the discounts are for each color sticker.)

1. How much does the first novel cost?

2. How much does the history book cost?

In buy-one-get-one-free sales, you will usually get the item that is cheaper for free. You will have to pay for the one that is more expensive.

3. Which book will she get for free? How much will she pay for both books?

4. How much money does she save in total with the discounts and the buy-one-get-one-free deal?

Now Mikayla looks at the buy-one-get-one-half-off shelf. On that shelf, Mikayla can only find one book she really wants to read, a novel that costs $14.50 and has a green sticker on it. She feels like she should buy something else, though, so she can take advantage of the deal. She sees a craft book she sort of wants, which is $19.25 and has a yellow sticker.

5. How much does the novel cost?

6. How much would buying both books cost? Mikayla will get half off of the book that costs less.

7. Do you think she should buy both books? Why or why not?

12
GROCERY SHOPPING: UNIT PRICE

Mikayla goes grocery shopping with her dad the next day. While at the grocery store, he teaches Mikayla about something called unit price. He uses the unit price all the time to figure out which foods are better values, and which he should buy.

You can find the unit price of a food usually in the upper left part of the shelf label, often highlighted in orange. It tells you how much the food is per unit. The unit is a measurement that varies from food to food. The unit could be pounds, ounces, liters, gallons, or something else.

The best unit prices are the cheapest. They show what the best buy will be, in terms of price. Unit prices are especially helpful if you are trying to compare two brands of the same food and want to get the one that is truly cheaper. If you're trying to save money at the grocery store, unit prices are really helpful!

The equation for unit price is:

$$\text{cost} \div \text{quantity (in units)}$$

For example, Mikayla and her dad take a look at the cereal aisle. They see one 24-ounce box of cereal for $3.69 and one 36-ounce box for $4.89.

Which one is the better deal? Which one will give them more ounces of cereal for a lower price? They need to find the unit price for each one. The equation for the 24-ounce box looks like this. Find the answer:

1. $3.69 ÷ 24 ounces =

2. What is the unit price for the second box?

Now compare the two unit prices. The one that is lower is the better deal. Mikayla and her dad will pay less for the same amount of cereal.

3. Which one is the better deal?

Sometimes, like in that example, an item that looks more expensive in price will be a better deal. But you're paying less per ounce than the option that looks cheaper.

Often, food in **bulk** will have a better unit price. You have to buy a lot of food, but it will be cheaper per unit than food you buy in smaller packages. If you know how to shop smart, you can save money.

Try another example. Mikayla wants to buy some almonds. She heads over to the nut shelf and sees that a package of almonds is $5.99. She looks at the back of the package and sees there are 8 ounces of almonds in the package.

Then she goes to the bulk section to look at almonds. Those almonds are $7.99 a pound. Which almonds should she buy if she wants 8 ounces?

You will need to find the unit price in cost per ounces. There are 16 ounces in a pound, so you are comparing 8 ounces of almonds at $5.99 and 16 ounces of almonds at $7.99.

4. Which ones have a cheaper unit price? Which ones should she buy?

Buy One, Get One Free

SAVE 50¢ ON TWO

SAVE

$

SAV

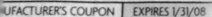
MANUFACTURER'S COUPON | EXPIRES 1/31/08

AVE 2.00

$5.00 OFF

This coupon may also be red
during
dine-in or

Not valid with any other offer. Tax an
Not for resale. Duplicated coupons

13
COUPONS

Mikayla's dad has brought along some coupons to the grocery store. He clipped them out of the newspaper, and he also found a couple online. Coupons are like discounts you carry around in your pocket. The items in the store might not be advertised as on sale, but if you have a coupon, you can still get a discount.

Mikayla's dad has several coupons. He wants to match them up to the food he's buying and see how much he is going to save. You can do the math too, on the next page.

Here are all the coupons he brought with him to the grocery store:

cereal, 30% off
juice, buy-one-get-one-free
bread, 20% off two loaves
canned green beans, 10% off
frozen berries, buy one get one 40% off

And here's what he actually bought:

2 boxes cereal, $4.89 each
2 bottles juice, $2.70 each
8 ounces almonds, $4.05
2 loaves bread, $2.20 each
1 can green beans, $.99
2 bags frozen berries, $4.50 each
6 oranges, $.78 each

Fill in this chart to keep track of everything he bought, and all the coupons:

Item	Amount	Original price (each)	Coupon	Price for all after coupon
Cereal	2 boxes	$4.89	30% off	$6.85

1. What was the total that Mikayla's dad paid at the cash register?

14
ONLINE SHOPPING

Mikayla has done a lot of shopping in stores lately. She needs some school supplies, but she doesn't really feel like going out to the store again. Instead, she orders what she needs online.

Online shopping can make life easier. All you have to do is search on your computer for exactly what you need, and then have it sent directly to your door. A lot of the same rules that apply to shopping in stores also apply to shopping online. And you also have to remember you'll pay a little extra for having it sent to you. This extra cost is called "shipping." However, you might be able to find cheaper items online than in the store if you search hard enough.

Mikayla has $23 in cash. She will have to use her mom's debit card to buy her school supplies online, because she doesn't have one of her own. She doesn't want to owe her mom too much money, though, so she is trying to stick to her budget.

She needs three notebooks, three folders, some pens, a binder, and a schedule planner. These are the options she finds online:

notebook, $3
folder, $.75
package of pens, $4.80
binder, $1.95
planner, $6.99

1. How much does everything cost?

2. How much does everything cost with the 7.3% sales tax added on?

Mikayla puts everything in her shopping cart online and goes to the checkout. As she's checking out, she realizes she forgot about shipping! She sees the shipping rates listed:

    total order $0–$10: $3.99
    total order $10.01–$20: $4.99
    total order $20.01–$50.00: $5.99

3. How much will she have to pay in shipping?

4. How much is her total order? Will she owe her mom any money?

15

PUTTING IT ALL TOGETHER

Mikayla has done a lot of shopping over the last few weeks. She has also used a lot of math to figure out budgets, determine her size in clothes, calculate sale prices, use unit prices, and more. See if you can remember some of the shopping math Mikayla has used, and which you can use too when you go shopping.

1. If you make $40 a week and you want to save 75% of it each week, how much do you have left over to spend?

2. A parking lot is 200 feet long and 180 feet wide. What is its area in square feet?

3. A video game you want to buy is $35.60. What will the sales tax be on it if the tax in your state is 8%?

   How much will the video game cost with tax?

4. You have $13 left in your checking account in the bank, and you have to keep at least $5 in there at all times. Can you afford to buy a chocolate bar that costs $1.54 and a game that costs $10.50?

5. What European size jeans would someone wear if her waist were 38 inches in circumference?

   What size juniors' clothes would she wear?

6. What is the cost-per-wear if you buy a sweater for $34.80 and wear it 73 times?

7. You are looking at a bunch of DVDs that are buy-one-get-one-half-off. You find two you want—one is $13.50 and the other is $17. How much will you spend on both of them?

8. You are trying to decide whether to buy a box of granola bars that are $3.99 for 6 bars, or another box that is $5.20 for 10 bars.

   Which should you buy, based on unit price (price per bar)?

9. You have a 25% off coupon for buying a video game that costs $12.80. How much will the game cost?

10. Your mother is letting you use her credit card to order a dress online that costs $33.99. She says you can't spend more than $40, and you figure you have plenty of money. But are you sure? Your sales tax is 7%, and the shipping is $3.50. Do you have enough money?

FIND OUT MORE IN BOOKS

Furgang, Kathy. *National Geographic Kids Everything Money*. Washington, D.C.: National Geographic Children's Books, 2013.

Minden, Cecilia. *Grocery Shopping by the Numbers*. North Mankato, Minn.: Cherry Lake Publishing, 2007.

Skrabanek, D.W. *Fractions, Decimals, and Percents*. Boston, Mass.: Steck-Vaughn School Supply, 2008.

Steffora, Tracey. *Math at the Store*. Portsmouth, N.H.: Heinemann, 2013.

FIND OUT MORE ON THE INTERNET

BrainPop: Comparing Prices
www.brainpop.com/math/dataanalysis/comparingprices

Cost-per-Wear Calculator
www.westfield.com.au/au/be-inspired/services/fashion-services/style-kit/cost-per-wear

Coupon Lingo Explained
www.savingcentswithsense.net/2009/04/coupon-lingo-explained

Hooda Math
www.hoodamath.com/games/shop.php

Math at the Mall
www.mathplayground.com/mathatthemall1.html

Unit Prices
www.studyzone.org/mtestprep/math8/a/unit_price7l.cfm

GLOSSARY

Approximately: not exact but fairly close; a good guess.

Bulk: a lot; a big amount.

Convert: to change to.

Correspond: to go along with or to match up with something.

Equivalents: things that are the same as one another.

Estimates: close guesses about something.

Deposits: puts something in.

Fee: money charged for the use of something.

Finances: the management of money.

Income: the money you make.

Manage: to organize; to be in charge of.

Multiples: numbers that can be divided by other numbers without remainders.

Rate: how quickly something happens.

Savings account: a bank service that keeps money you want to save rather than spend.

Value: how much something is worth, in money, time, or other things.

Withdraw: to take out.

Answers

1.

1. $65
2. $90
3. $87.27
4. The headphones were the closest ($.14 off) and the movie was the farthest off ($3.25).

2.

1. $50.44
2. $64
3. $25.60
4. Yes ($25.60 x 2 = $51.20)
5. No, she can't afford to buy either of them.

3.

1. Length = (14 x 12) +9 = 177 inches, Width = (6 x 12) +2 = 74 inches.
2. A = 177 x 74 = 13,098 square inches
3. 24 inches
4. 24 + 74 = 98 inches
5. A = 177 x 98 = 17,346 square inches; the new area is 4,248 square inches larger.

4.

1. Yes, she has $63.95
2. .073
3. $4.38
4. X= $4.38
5. $64.38; no she can't quite afford it.

5.

1. ($31.50) + ($31.50 x .073) = $33.80
2. $7.05

3. $63.95 – $33.80 – $7 = $23.15
4. $.95; Yes (the total will be $13.94)
5. No, she needs to give her $.26 more.
6. She has $9.21 left, so yes, she has enough.

6.

1. $28.79
2. $20
3. $23.50; no, she doesn't have enough money.
4. Afford: board game, wallet; Not afford: shirt, computer case

7.

1. No, he can't pay for any so he will need to use his credit card.
2. Suit 1, Suit 3, Suit 4, and Suit 5
3. None.
4. Suit 1, Suit 3, and Suit 5.
5. $105.60 + ($105.60 x .073) = $113.31
   ($80 + $95) – ($25 + $25) – $113.31 = $11.69

8.

1. 6 and 8
2. 36 and 37

9.

1. $2 per wear
2. Pair 2, Pair 1, Pair 3
3. $.24 per wear
4. Pair 2: $1.21 per wear, Pair 3: $.63
5. Pair 1, because they are cheapest cost-per-wear.

10.

1. $6
2. $15

3. $3, because 90% off is a big discount and means a lot of money will be taken off the price.
4. $16 – ($16 x .9) = $1.60

11.

1. $23 – ($23 x .75) = $5.75
2. $14 – ($14 x .10) = $12.60
3. She will get the first novel for free; she will pay $12.60 for both books.
4. She will save $24.40
5. $14.50 ÷ 2 = $7.25
6. $19.25 – ($19.25 x .25) + ($7.25 ÷ 2) = $18.06
7. Probably not. She would only spend $7.25 if she bought the novel she really wanted, but she would spend $18.06 if she bought both books.

12.

1. $.15 per ounce
2. $4.89 ÷ 16 = $.14 per ounce
3. The second box with 36 ounces
4. Packaged: $5.99 ÷ 8 ounces = $.75; Bulk: $7.99 ÷ 16 ounces= $.50; she should buy the bulk almonds.

13.

1. $29.89

Item	Amount	Original price (each)	Coupon	Price for all after coupon
Cereal	2 boxes	$4.89	30% off	$6.85
Juice	2 bottles	$2.70	buy-one-get-one-free	$2.70
Almonds	8 ounces	$4.05	none	$4.05
Bread	2 loaves	$2.20	20% off	$3.52
Green beans	1 can	$.99	10% off	$.89
Frozen berries	2 bags	$4.50	buy-one-get-one 40% off	$7.20
Oranges	6	$.78	none	$4.68

14.

1. $24.99
2. $24.99 + ($24.99 x .073) = $26.81
3. $5.99
4. $32.80; yes, she will owe her mom money.

15.

1. $40 – ($40 x .75) = $10
2. 200 x 180 = 36,000 square feet
3. $2.85; $38.45
4. No, you will be spending more than $8.
5. Size 38; 11
6. $.48
7. $23.75
8. Buy the second box ($3.99 ÷ 6 = $.67 per bar or $5.20 ÷ 10 = $.52 per bar).
9. $9.60
10. Yes. The dress, shipping, and sales tax added together comes to $39.87.

INDEX

ABOUT THE AUTHOR

Helen Thompson lives in upstate New York. She worked first as a social worker and then became a teacher as her second career.

Picture Credits